P9-DXL-001

Nighty Night,

ZooBorns

by Andrew Bleiman and Chris Eastland

Most of the photos in this book were previously published in *ZooBorns: The Newest, Cutest Animals from the World's Zoos and Aquariums*; *ZooBorns Cats!: The Newest, Cutest Kittens and Cubs from the World's Zoos*; and *ZooBorns: The Next Generation: Newer, Cuter, More Exotic Animals from the World's Zoos and Aquariums*.

Ready-to-Read

Simon Spotlight
New York   London   Toronto   Sydney   New Delhi

SIMON SPOTLIGHT

An imprint of Simon & Schuster Children's Publishing Division

1230 Avenue of the Americas, New York, New York 10020

Text copyright © 2013 by ZooBorns LLC

Photos copyright © 2010, 2011, 2012, 2013 by ZooBorns LLC

Most of the photos in this book were previously published in *ZooBorns: The Newest, Cutest Animals from the World's Zoos and Aquariums*; *ZooBorns Cats!: The Newest, Cutest Kittens and Cubs from the World's Zoos*; and *ZooBorns: The Next Generation: Newer, Cuter, More Exotic Animals from the World's Zoos and Aquariums*.

For information about special discounts for bulk purchases, please contact Simon & Schuster Special Sales at 1-866-506-1949 or business@simonandschuster.com.

The Simon & Schuster Speakers Bureau can bring authors to your live event. For more information or to book an event contact the Simon & Schuster Speakers Bureau at 1-866-248-3049 or visit our website at www.simonspeakers.com.

Manufactured in the United States of America 0613 LAK

First Edition

10 9 8 7 6 5 4 3 2 1

Library of Congress Cataloging-in-Publication Data

Bleiman, Andrew.

Nighty Night, ZooBorns / by Andrew Bleiman and Chris Eastland.

p. cm. — (Ready-to-read)

"Most of the photos in this book were previously published in *ZooBorns: The Newest, Cutest Animals from the World's Zoos and Aquariums*; *ZooBorns Cats!: The Newest, Cutest Kittens and Cubs from the World's Zoos*; and *ZooBorns: The Next Generation: Newer, Cuter, More Exotic Animals from the World's Zoos and Aquariums*."

ISBN 978-1-4424-4386-0 (pbk. : alk. paper) — ISBN 978-1-4424-4385-3 (hardcover : alk. paper) — ISBN 978-1-4424-4387-7 (ebook) 1. Zoo animals—Infancy—Juvenile literature. 2. Sleep behavior in animals—Juvenile literature. I. Eastland, Chris. II. Title.

QL77.5.B5389 2013

591.3'92073—dc23

2012020356

Welcome to the wonderful world of
ZooBorns!

The newborn animals featured in this book live
in zoos around the world. Get to know them through
adorable photos and fun facts written in language that
is just right for emerging readers. Your child might not
be able to pronounce all the animal species names yet,
but if you stay close by, you can help sound them out.

This book can also be used as a tool to begin a
conversation about endangered species. The more
we learn about animals in zoos, the more we can do
to protect animals in the wild. Please visit your
local accredited zoo or aquarium to learn more!

Note to readers: Some of the animals in this book are
nocturnal, which means that they are awake at night and
asleep during the day. But that does not mean we cannot
say "nighty night" to them when it is their bedtime.

Kito is a Hamadryas baboon.
At night, baboons, like Kito,
snuggle with hundreds
of other baboons.

That is a big slumber party!
Nighty night, baby baboon.

Siku, the polar bear cub, loves to play on the ice. At bedtime he loves sleeping on his warm blanket.

Nighty night,
baby polar bear.

These snow leopards
do not need pajamas
to keep warm.
They wrap their tails around
their necks like scarves.

Nighty night, baby snow
leopards.

When it is time for bed, this Senegal bushbaby calls out to his friends, and they all cuddle up!

Nighty night,
baby bushbaby.

Red pandas love to eat bamboo leaves.

Right now these red pandas are ready for bed.

Nighty night, baby red pandas.

Ruth is a Hoffmann's
two-toed sloth.
Sloths move very slowly,
especially at bedtime!

Nighty night, baby sloth.

Look at Pepe yawn!
It is time for this maned
wolf pup to hit the hay.

Nighty night,
baby maned wolf.

Pan is not tired at all.

He is an aye-aye.

At night he looks for

grubs to eat.

But even Pan has to sleep.

He sleeps during the day!
Nighty night, baby aye-aye.

Zebras have stripes.
Kalispell has stripes too,
but he is not a zebra.
He is an okapi.
He is a sleepy okapi.

What will Kalispell
dream about?
Nighty night, baby okapi.

Blitz had a big day!
Now this Eurasian lynx
is tucked in tight
under the covers.
He wants a good-night kiss!

Nighty night, baby lynx.

Special thanks to the photographers and institutions that made ZooBorns! possible:

Cover:
ASIAN SMALL-CLAWED OTTER
Sheri Horiszny/Santa Barbara Zoo

HAMADRYAS BABOON
Kito
Julie Larsen Maher © WCS

HOFFMAN'S TWO-TOED SLOTH
Ruth
Amelia Beamish/Rosamond Gifford Zoo

POLAR BEAR
Siku
© Søren Koch/Hilmer &
Koch Nature Photography

MANED WOLF
Pepe
Tom Svensson/Norden's Ark

SNOW LEOPARD
Kira Victoria and Pasha Ryan
Ken Ardill

AYE-AYE
Pan
Dave Parsons/Denver Zoo

SENEGAL BUSHBABY
Ryan Hawk/Woodland Park Zoo

OKAPI
Kalispell
Dave Parsons/Denver Zoo

RED PANDA
Debbie Ryan/Cotswold Wildlife Park

EURASIAN LYNX
Blitz
Christian Sperka